W9-AFF-771

The SPORTS HEROES Library

Hockey's FEARLESS GOALIES

Nathan Aaseng

 Lerner Publications Company • Minneapolis

ACKNOWLEDGMENTS: The photographs are reproduced through the courtesy of: pp. 4, 7, 31, 72, 77, 78, Al Ruelle; pp. 10, 12, New York Islanders; pp. 14, 48, 53, 57, 58, 61, Bruce Bennett; pp. 16, 18, 19, 25, 42, 62, 64, 70, 71, 75, United Press International, Inc.; pp. 20, 23, New Jersey Devils; pp. 28, 33, 35 (Sol Benjamin), 36 (Sol Benjamin); p. 38, Toronto Maple Leafs (Robert B. Shaver); pp. 40, 44, Robert B. Shaver; p. 50, St. Louis Blues; pp. 67, 68, Vancouver Canucks; p. 74, Boston Bruins. Cover photograph by Al Ruelle.

LIBRARY OF CONGRESS CATALOGING IN PUBLICATION DATA

Aaseng, Nathan.
  Hockey's fearless goalies.

  (The Sports heroes library)
  Summary: Outlines the hockey careers of eight outstanding goalies: Billy Smith, Chico Resch, Tony Esposito, Mike Palmateer, Mike Liut, Andy Moog, Richard Brodeur, and Pete Peeters.
    1. Hockey — Goalkeepers — Biography — Juvenile literature. 2. National Hockey League — Juvenile literature. [1. Hockey players] I. Title. II. Series.
GV848.5.A1A247   1984   796.96′2′0922 [B] [920]
ISBN 0-8225-1341-2 (lib. bdg.)   83-17512

Manufactured in the United States of America

International Standard Book Number: 0-8225-1341-2
Library of Congress Catalog Card Number: 83-17512

1 2 3 4 5 6 7 8 9 10 93 92 91 90 89 88 87 86 85 84

Contents

Boston Bruin goalie Pete Peeters makes a living the hard way by getting his body in front of shots such as this one.

Introduction

Glenn Hall considered the game to be pure torture and often lost his dinner before going out to play. Roger Crozier developed ulcers by the age of 17. Wilf Cude's nerves were so shot that he once fired his steak, ketchup and all, at the wall. Jacques Plante lived in daily fear of a new ache or illness in his body and took up knitting to calm his nerves. These four men suffered through careers at one of the most miserable occupations ever invented: goalie in the National Hockey League.

To understand what a professional goaltender goes through, picture yourself standing on a baseball diamond halfway between the pitcher's mound and home plate. Think of what it would be like to try and stand there while a fastball pitcher like Nolan Ryan fired his warm-up pitches at you. Actually, goalies have had to block objects traveling even faster than a Ryan fastball. Hockey slapshots have been clocked at speeds nearly 20 miles per hour *faster* than the hardest pitch ever thrown!

When a hard rubber disc, three inches in diameter, one inch thick, and weighing about six ounces, comes at you that fast, it takes courage to hold your ground. Even though goalies wear so much padding they resemble teddy bears, there is still the matter of their exposed heads. Boston Bruin goalie Gary Cheevers used to draw stitches to mark where a puck had struck him during a game. By the end of the year, he usually ran out of room and had to start in on a new mask.

As if the danger were not enough, goalies rarely get any respect from fans *or* players. When Plante pioneered the face mask in the 1950s after breaking his cheekbone for the second time, hockey people scoffed at him for his lack of toughness. And although the face mask is now standard equipment for goalies, these men remain the team scapegoats. An entire team can play sloppy defense and all that will show up on the highlight film is a puck flying past a sprawling goalie. Even when goalies play flawlessly, other players have a way of downgrading their talents. A netminder who has played superbly is often described as having been "unconscious."

Although goalies rarely get the recognition that high scorers get, the pressure they face is far worse.

Goalies aren't paid to be graceful. Even while sprawled on the ice, Peeters kicks out another shot.

Experts will tell you that a top goalie can turn a bad team into a good one, while a poor goalie can destroy everything that a good team has worked for. A review of Stanley Cup winners over the years shows that one of the key ingredients to winning is having a capable goalie. Often just one great save can take the steam out of an attacking team and shake their confidence for the rest of the game. On the other hand, a fluke bounce on a long, easy shot can make a goalie look foolish and destroy *his* team's confidence.

7

It is no wonder that many of these human missiles have gained a reputation for being somewhat odd. It is understandable that the job could make one superstitious, high-strung, or worse. Some goalies have been so noted for strange behavior that even their own teammates walk a wide path around them.

Rating a goalie's performance is not an easy job. There is one major annual prize for goalies, the Vezina Trophy. Named after Georges Vezina, who tended goal for the Montreal Canadiens from 1911 to 1926, this prize honors the goalie or goalies who allow the fewest goals per game. But this statistic can be misleading. Those who play for strong defensive teams have an advantage over those who either concentrate more on offense or have generally poor teams. The number of saves can be a measure of a goalie's performance in a game, but even that does not tell you if they were easy or hard saves. A good goalie has to be seen to be appreciated.

This book takes a look at eight of the top goalies in the NHL. It would be difficult to imagine a wider variety of characters. But if Mike Palmateer or Billy Smith seem a bit strange, try to be sympathetic. After all, they are trying to survive at the craziest job in the world of sports!

1
Billy
Smith

The New York Islanders sat next to their lockers, muttering about that crazy, stick-swinging goalie. Rubbing their sore shin bones, they agreed that something ought to be done about him. There's nothing unusual in a team griping about a goalie. The area directly in front of the net, the crease, has long been a battleground between forwards looking to screen the goalie from the shot and goalies trying to drive them away. What made this scene different was that the Islanders were talking about their own goalie, Billy Smith!

Battlin' Billy has gained a reputation as the most ornery goalie in the game. Even his teammates have learned to keep their heads up when cruising around the net in practice. At the same time,

Battlin' Billy doesn't even flinch as the puck clips him on the right shoulder.

though, the Islanders have been glad to see Billy wearing their orange and blue uniform. During the 1980s, Smith has established himself as the NHL's best, as well as its most talked-about, play-off goalie.

Billy was born in Perth, Ontario (a town of about 5,000), in 1950. His father, an immigrant from Northern Ireland, quickly grew fond of the Canadian national sport. He coached his boys during their younger days and spared no effort to see that they got a chance to practice hockey. He painted houses to get money for equipment, shoveled snow off the backyard rink before going to work, and strung lights over the rink so his sons could practice at night. Being the youngest of the Smith boys, Billy was elected to be the goalie.

At first Smith spent more time minding the bench than minding the goal. After joining the Smith Falls junior league team at the age of 14, he spent three full seasons as a backup goalie. In 1969-70, though, he moved on to the Cornwall Royals, where he was given a chance to play. The Los Angeles Kings drafted him that year and assigned him to Springfield of the American Hockey League. After helping Springfield to the championship, Billy was brought up to the Kings for a trial.

Los Angeles had had trouble keeping the puck

Billy Smith

out of its end, and Billy's statistics did not look impressive. But Bill Torrey, general manager of the newly formed New York Islanders, liked what he saw of the young man. He took note of one game in which Billy and the Kings were losing, 8-1. Despite the hopeless situation, Smith refused to quit, and he played the final minutes as intensely as ever. That was the kind of player that Torrey wanted, and he claimed Billy for the Islanders in the 1972 expansion draft.

For a number of years, Smith shared goaltending

duties with Chico Resch. The two were close in talent and developed a friendly rivalry. Neither took offense when first one and then the other appeared to be taking over the top spot in goal. Smith's relation with his other teammates, however, was not always so polite. Although pleasant and easygoing off the ice, Billy was deadly serious when it came to goaltending. If teammates were getting in his way while he was trying to block a shot, he would thump them on the legs with his stick. If they wanted to fight, Billy would fight. If they wanted to keep firing hard shots at him in practice, he would leave the net.

But Billy was far tougher on opponents than on his teammates. It didn't take long before Battlin' Billy had become the most penalized goalie in the game. The fiery little netminder (5 feet, 9 inches and 170 pounds) also warned his teammates not to come to his aid in a fight. Despite his size, he was determined to fight his own battles, even against the biggest men in the game. His habit of pounding on shins with his stick made him more enemies than anyone else in the NHL. He insisted that if referees refused to protect him by calling interference penalties, he would protect himself as best he could.

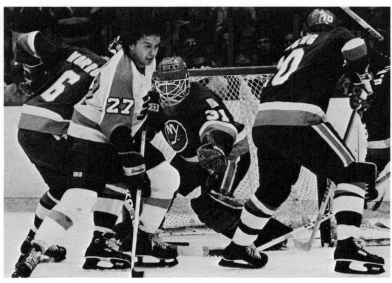

Staying cool under pressure, Smith tries to find the loose puck before Philadelphia Flyer sharpshooter Reggie Leach (27) can put it in the net.

Smith's style of goaltending was so aggressive that most players didn't know what to make of him. During one game, an opponent broke away from the Islander defensemen and moved in, unguarded, for a shot at Smith. Rather than wait for the fakes, Smith skated out of his net towards the attacker. To the delight of the astonished fans, Smith knocked the man off the puck with a crunching body check.

Smith also made no secret of the fact that he wanted to be the first NHL goalie to score a goal. His big moment finally came in 1979, completely by accident. Trailing New York by one goal in the final minute, the Colorado Rockies replaced their goalie with an extra attacker. The Rockies then swarmed around the Islander net. Billy blocked one shot, but the rebound went to a Colorado player who passed it back out to the point men. Unfortunately, the puck got by them and slid all the way into the Colorado net! Since Smith was the last Islander to touch the puck, he was given credit for the goal.

It was later that year that Smith earned applause for his play-off work. The greater the Stanley Cup pressure, the better Billy played. His style was difficult to attack because he didn't have one particular method. Against some teams, he concentrated on guarding against high shots and, against others, he was watchful for low ones. No two teams agreed on how to shoot against Smith because there was no predicting how he would play.

After getting past the Buffalo Sabres in the semi-finals, the Islanders challenged the top-rated Philadelphia Flyers for the Stanley Cup in 1980. The teams were almost identical in style and skill, and many agreed that the edge in New York's four-games-to-two victory had come from the fine play of Smith.

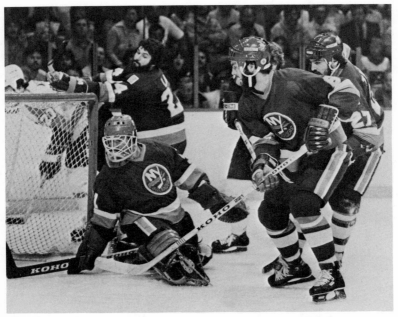

By clearing the Flyers from scoring position, Islander defensemen
made Smith's job easier in this 1980 Stanley Cup final.

The next season, Smith and the Islanders were
almost unbeatable in the play-offs. Smith won 14
of the 17 Stanley Cup games in which he started
to help his club repeat as champions. The Islanders
teased Smith at play-off time, saying his idea of
a good practice was standing and watching the
others sweat. But they knew when a key save was
needed, Billy would be there.

The New York Rangers were putting up a stiff
fight against their crosstown rivals in 1982, and

they trailed only three games to two in their play-off series. In game six, the Rangers outskated the Islanders but still trailed, 4-3, thanks to Smith's acrobatics. With three minutes to go, the Rangers swarmed around the net. A series of crisp passes left Reijo Ruotsalainen open about 10 feet in front of the net. He fired at the wide-open cage, but Billy flew across the crease and grabbed the puck just before falling back into the net. Billy called it his best save ever, and it ended the Rangers' chance for an upset. The final two series that year were no contest as Billy and the Islanders swept Quebec and Vancouver to earn their third straight Stanley Cup title.

Just when it seemed that Battlin' Billy had calmed down during the 1982-83 season, he charged back into the spotlight. There was no mistaking the old Billy Smith when he took a few whacks at the Edmonton Oilers during the finals. After Smith was called for slashing stars Glen Anderson and Wayne Gretzky, the Edmonton press raged against him. But the name-calling and threats of violence only spurred Smith on to his best effort ever. The Oilers, who had scored an NHL record of 424 goals during the year and had destroyed their rivals in earlier play-off rounds, could not get the puck past Smith.

Edmonton center Ken Linseman has wandered into Smith's territory in the 1983 Stanley Cup final. Billy offers his usual welcome.

Billy shut out the Oilers in their own rink to win the first game, 2-0. Although Edmonton outshot New York in every game, the Islanders easily swept the series. The stunned Wayne Gretzky had not managed a single goal against Smith, and the entire

Edmonton team got only six goals in the four games!

Typically, Billy was not particularly gracious in victory. Instead of expressing joy over winning the Conn Smythe Award as the most valuable player in the play-offs, Smith could only fume to reporters about all the abuse he had taken in the series. Reporters as well as the Edmonton Oilers learned what Islander captain Denis Potvin had once said about Smith: "You don't handle Billy Smith; you have to give him room."

Billy Smith, the Most Valuable Player of the play-offs, frustrated Wayne Gretzky (99), the MVP of the regular season.

Chico Resch is much busier playing for the last-place New Jersey
Devils than he was as a goalie for the Islanders.

2
Glenn
"Chico" Resch

After reading about the grim warfare in the world of Billy Smith, it's a good time to look at the lighter side of goaltending. For that you only have to go as far as Smith's goaltending buddy of many years, Chico Resch. Other than a common skill at stopping pucks, the two were total opposites. Smith was the serious fighter; Resch the happy-go-lucky leader. Recently their careers have taken them to the extremes of the hockey world as well. While Smith has been surrounded by the best group of players in the NHL, Resch has been playing with the worst.

Just about everything in Chico's life has been colorful, starting with the name of his 1948 birthplace: Moose Jaw, Saskatchewan. Like many Canadian youngsters, Resch was given skates and a hockey stick at the age of three. There are those, however, who would question whether or not his father had Chico's best interests at heart. After all, the plan was to make a goalie out of the little guy! Little Glenn followed his dad and uncle to the basement where they set up apple carts for a goal. Then they proceeded to take shots at Glenn in the goal.

Resch proved to be a tough little goalie. In his younger days, he refused to even wear a face mask. But a hard shot changed both his mind and his appearance. After losing a tooth to a hockey puck at the age of 12, Resch saw the sense in wearing some protection.

Although many top athletes have found success after frightful beginnings, few can claim to have struggled out of as deep a hole as Chico. You can't get much lower than third-string goalie on a last-place team in the Saskatchewan junior leagues, so Resch decided to escape the competitive junior hockey ranks to attend an American college. He chose the University of Minnesota-Duluth, a small state school with a good hockey program.

After four years of netminding for the UMD Bulldogs, Resch had become better equipped to handle his position. The Montreal Canadiens showed

Glenn "Chico" Resch

interest in him and sent him to a minor league team in Muskegon, Michigan. As Resch toiled away in the minors, he saw that the Canadiens had no room for him on their roster, and he was afraid that soon he would be too old to get a chance to play in the NHL. When the New York Islanders claimed him in 1972, it seemed like a lucky break. But it just brought more insult, as even the pitiful Islanders turned their backs on him. After two more years of play in New Haven and Fort Worth, Chico finally earned a two-game trial with the Islanders in 1973, and he made the team the next year.

As a 26-year-old rookie, Resch was older than many of the Islander veterans. New York still had their doubts about him, and Chico played in only 25 games during his first season. Although he came through with three shutouts and a fine 2.47 goals-allowed average in those contests, he still found himself on the bench for the play-offs. Only when things seemed hopeless did he finally get the call. The Islanders had lost the first three games of their best-of-seven series with the Pittsburgh Penguins. The defense had been especially shaky as Pittsburgh scored 14 goals in the three games. Only once had a team come back to win a Stanley Cup series after trailing three games to none. And that had been back in 1942 when the Toronto Maple Leafs had done it to the Detroit Red Wings.

The confident Penguins took aim at Resch in game four and kept the pressure on for the full 60 minutes. But the chatty goalie got in the way of almost everything. He made 37 saves in holding off Pittsburgh and posting a 3-1 win. In the next game, Pittsburgh peppered Chico with 38 shots. This time he stopped all but 2 in a 4-2 victory.

By this time, the Penguins had begun to feel edgy as well as frustrated by some bad luck. Many of their shots had come within an inch of scoring

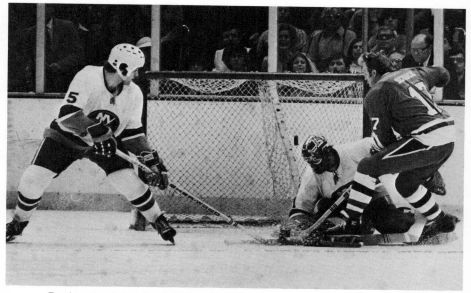

During the Islanders' 1975 play-off miracle, Resch needed no help from the goal posts to stop Pittsburgh's Ron Schock.

only to bounce off one of the goal posts. Chico delighted the crowd by taking off his mask and kissing the post after one close call. It was no laughing matter to the Penguins, however, as they put only one puck in the net in a 4-1 loss that tied the series.

Resch finished his incredible show by completely destroying the Penguins' Stanley Cup dreams as he shut them out, 1-0, to put the Islanders in the record book. After the game, Resch put on a show almost as good as the one he had given on the ice. Noting that nine Pittsburgh shots had clanged off the posts in the last four games, he nominated the goal posts as the series' most valuable player!

The 5-foot, 9-inch, 165-pounder had become one of the most popular players in the NHL. Unlike his netminding partner, Smith, Resch avoided looking for trouble. But although quite harmless on the ice, Chico still filled the role of leader. He worked with teammates on their defense and shouted instructions to the players on the ice. But Resch couldn't be deadly serious, even at game time. Unlike most goalies who concentrated so well that they barely noticed the crowd, Resch would sometimes perform for the crowd. He would wave and raise his stick to them to let them know how he was doing. And while the demands of goaltending gave others queasy stomachs, Resch had no trouble eating. He loved a big meal of spaghetti, ice cream, and soda before a game.

Resch's best statistics came in 1975-76 when he recorded seven shutouts and a 2.07 goals-against average. Continuing to shine in the play-offs, he allowed only 2.08 goals per game in 1977, but his team still bowed out early. He and Smith continued to share the duties evenly until the 1980 play-offs. After Smith's starring role in New York's first

Stanley Cup win that year, they felt they no longer needed Chico and sent him to Colorado in March of 1981.

At Colorado Resch found plenty of action as he played in more games and faced an enormous barrage of shots. With the Islanders, he had grown used to facing about 25 shots. The Rockies' defense normally let about 35 shots fly towards the net, but Resch didn't let the lack of support affect his play. Although a player on a last-place team rarely gets noticed, Resch still placed fourth in the All-Star voting in 1982. The next year, Chico continued to provide good saves and good humor when the team moved to New Jersey, and in December he earned his first shutout as a Devil in a 2-0 victory against the North Stars. There, while waiting patiently for the Devils to avoid the cellar, Resch could take satisfaction in one thing: If things were bad for the team now, think how hopeless they would be without him!

Tony Esposito, Chicago's ageless wonder

3
Tony
Esposito

Younger brothers all over the world would understand what Tony Esposito has gone through. Growing up in Sault Sainte Marie, Ontario, in the 1940s, he had to take a back seat to his older brother, Phil. Even when it came to his favorite sport, hockey, Tony had to put up with the misfortune of being younger. When he played hockey in the basement with Phil, he would have to let Phil take the starring role. Phil got to shoot the rolled-up sock at the goal; Tony's job was to stop it.

The two continued at those positions as they moved up through the ranks of boys' hockey in Canada. But while Phil showed a special talent as a goal scorer, Tony didn't see much hope for himself. Rather than struggle in the junior leagues in hopes of a hockey career, he thought it wiser to go to college. He hadn't totally given up on hockey, though, and attended Michigan Tech, a school with a strong hockey program.

Tony played well during his college years, and when he graduated in 1967, the Montreal Canadiens showed interest in him. After spending nearly two full seasons in a minor league, Tony got a chance to play in the NHL late in the 1968-69 season. Injuries to Canadien goalies had forced Montreal to start Tony in 13 games. With two shut-outs and a 2.73 goals-allowed average in those contests, he proved he was ready for the big time.

Tony's performance clogged up the already crowded Montreal goaltending ranks. With a blend of wiley old Gump Worsely, new star Rogatien Vachon, and bright prospect Phil Myre already on hand, Tony felt as useful as a second spare tire. The last-place Chicago Black Hawks, however, were happy to take any leftovers from the power-ful Canadiens. They traded for Esposito and gave him a chance at the starting job in 1969-70.

While Tony was struggling to earn a spot in the NHL, brother Phil had already made a name for himself with his shooting. The older Esposito, who had just earned his first scoring title in 1969 with

30

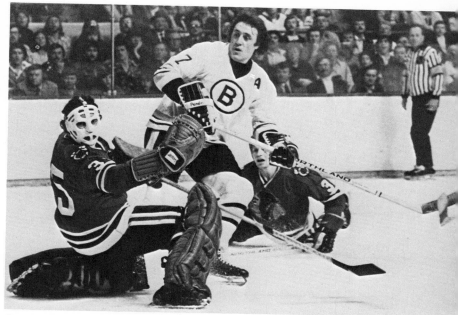

Even as a pro, Tony was picked on by his big brother. Here Tony can only hope that Phil Esposito (7) has shot wide of the net.

the Boston Bruins, did not make Tony's task any easier. Those hours of practice in the basement paid off for Phil in the brothers' first NHL meeting. Phil scored both of his team's goals in a 2-2 tie. During the game, their rivalry caused confusion for their parents. One minute they would be rooting for Phil to score, and then they were scolding Phil for scoring on his brother. While proud of all that Phil had accomplished, they hoped that Tony could have some success as well.

As it turned out, there was no need for their parents to worry. Esposito plugged the holes in the Black Hawk defense. Playing in 63 games in 1969-70, he held the opposition to only 2.17 goals per game. When Tony was especially sharp, opponents may as well have been shooting at a wall. Posting an incredible 15 shutouts, Tony broke the NHL record of 13, which Harry Lumley had set back in 1953-54. Tony's play turned the standings upside down as the Black Hawks jumped from last place in the Eastern Conference to first place. That year Tony proudly added two trophies to the family collection, a pair that Phil could never collect. He earned the Calder Cup as the NHL's best rookie and the Vezina Trophy for outstanding goalie.

Despite all of the evidence, there were those who insisted that Tony wasn't playing his position correctly. Rather than play the standard stand-up style, Tony was known as a "flopper." That meant he often went down to his knees to make saves, and he dove and flopped around from one side of the net to the other. This kind of style supposedly left too much of the net open for rebounds, and word spread throughout the league that Esposito could be beaten on shots to the upper corners. Some thought that Tony had done well only because

Tony Esposito

he was one of the few goalies who caught with his right hand. Once players got used to him, they could be expected to score more often.

Tony heard these criticisms for many years, but he never changed the way he played. Doing things his own way, he again helped Chicago to first place in 1970-71, this time as a member of the Western Division. Trying to bring the Stanley Cup to Chicago, Esposito played in every Black Hawk play-off game that spring. His club did make the finals and battled the Montreal Canadiens through a tough, seven-game series. Tony allowed just over two goals per game in the play-offs, but Chicago fell short of the Cup by a single goal in the seventh game.

The Black Hawks rewarded Tony with some time off the next season. With newly acquired Gary Smith easing the goaltending load, Tony was harder to crack than a bank vault. His average of 1.76 goals allowed per game easily ran off with another Vezina Trophy.

Throughout the 1970s, Chicago never had to worry about their goaltending as the durable Esposito came through time and again. In 1973 he again took them to the Stanley Cup finals, and, the following year, he captured his third Vezina with a 2.04 average and 10 shutouts. He still couldn't win any points for style, however. The 5-foot, 11-inch, 185-pound star seemed bulky and awkward in his pads. No one could get him to change his scrambling style, which sometimes made him look like a fish out of water. But hockey players had learned that looks were deceiving. They knew that Tony had two of the fastest hands in the business as well as a sixth sense that seemed to put him in the right spot at the right time.

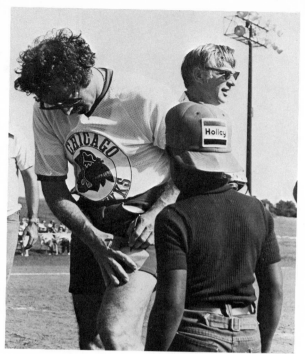

Goalies are used to getting abuse, not admiration, so Tony may have been a little surprised that this boy actually wanted an autograph.

Tony's quiet personality kept him from being as well known as his high-scoring brother. While Phil liked to talk and crack jokes, Tony insisted that there was nothing funny about his job. It took intense concentration and left no time for entertaining crowds with showmanship. Tony took the game so seriously that he could not eat within seven hours of an approaching game. But the concentration paid off as Tony could often figure out what would happen long before the plays unfolded.

35

This may not be the classic goal-tending style, but Tony has shown that he can get the job done.

Despite the fact that he hasn't always played on the most talented teams, Esposito could proudly claim that he had helped his team to nine first-place finishes in his career. During most of that time, he had little rest from his duties. Even in 1979-80, when some were suggesting that he was starting to slow down, Tony played in more games (69) than any other goalie in the league. His rivals certainly weren't fooled by reports that Tony was on his last leg. In a poll taken before the 1980-81 season, the players voted him the best goalie in the NHL.

With the Black Hawks rebuilding in 1981-82 and his goals-against average up to 3.75, there were more suggestions that Tony should retire. But he came back in May to give the lowly Hawks a boost in their surprising Stanley Cup showing. It was his 2-0 shutout of the St. Louis Blues that put the Black Hawks into their semifinal match against the Vancouver Canucks. Still going strong in 1983, Esposito shared duties with Murray Bannerman as Chicago claimed yet another first-place divisional finish. Of course, it's easy to see why 39-year-old Tony keeps going. When his older brother retired in 1981, Tony had his parents' undivided attention when he played. After all those years in Phil's shadow, he deserved it!

No, it's not an Aztec warrior. It's just Mike Palmateer out for an evening of fun and adventure.

4
Mike
Palmateer

It may have been lucky that Mike Palmateer found work as a professional goalie. If he hadn't, he probably would have been eaten by sharks or broken his neck falling off some sheer cliff while hunting for thrills. As it is, sticking his face in the path of screaming slap shots provides *almost* all that he needs to satisfy his huge taste for danger.

Mike, born in 1954, is a native of Toronto, Ontario. Of the six Palmateer children, Mike was the one who always went out looking for adventure. Sometimes he would just read about it. As a youngster, he loved to read stories of the Hardy Boys, and, when that got dull, he moved into the world of James Bond. Then there were the times when Mike chose to act out his adventures. On one family vacation by the ocean, his

Mike Palmateer

worried parents found their missing boy out in a boat. Naturally, he was trying to find sharks!

Mike's fearless attitude and his small size made him a good candidate for goalie. But at the same time, Mike liked to do some skating and scoring of his own. Until the age of 17, he played goalie for a team in one league and forward in another. This offensive experience helped him in his net-minding duties, allowing him to recognize plays as they developed. Whether Palmateer was guarding the nets or attacking them, he never played on a losing team in his growing-up years. To top off his junior career, he led the Toronto Marlboros to the Junior A title in 1974.

Never one to lack confidence, Mike assumed that most of the NHL teams would be fighting for his services. But a minor knee injury had dropped Palmateer a few notches in the scouts' ratings, so it wasn't until the fifth round of the 1974 draft that he was claimed by his hometown team, the Toronto Maple Leafs. Mike was so stunned that he has called it the biggest disappointment of his life.

Fighting off his discouragement, Palmateer worked his way up to the Maple Leafs in 1976. The team fell into a seven-game losing streak and finally called on Mike to bail them out. He came through with a classy effort in a 3-1 win that put Toronto back on the winning road. The rookie went on to allow only 3.21 goals per game and shut out four opponents. The next season, Mike was even more spectacular. With five shutouts to his credit, Mike lowered his average to 2.74. With such solid work in the nets, Toronto won 41 games to tie their team record for victories in a season.

It was the misfortune of the New York Islanders to find that Mike had more in store that season. The Islanders, who had breezed to first place in

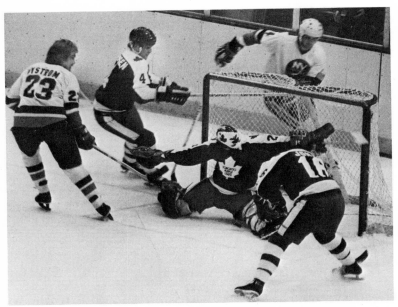

Even the point-blank shot by New York's Bob Nystrom (23) couldn't get past Palmateer as the little goalie shocked the Islanders in the 1978 play-offs.

their division with a 48-17-15 record, were expected to polish off the Maple Leafs in their drive for the 1978 Stanley Cup. But the 5-foot, 9-inch, 170-pound Palmateer kicked away so many shots that he sent Islanders muttering back to the bench. New York's famous scoring line of Bryan Trottier, Mike Bossy, and Clark Gillies couldn't find any weakness in the defense. Palmateer blunted the Islander attack and allowed only 13 goals in the seven-game series as Toronto sprung the upset.

Islander coach Al Arbour called it the greatest display of goaltending he had ever seen.

The credit for Mike's success was due largely to his extraordinary reflexes. He once had someone flip 10 pucks in the air at once as he skated past. Mike collected 5 of them before they hit the ice! But Palmateer was not above seeking help from good luck charms. For example, he had a habit of eating popcorn before games. It was a practice that went back to his peewee days when he didn't have time for a full supper before practice. While with the Maple Leafs, Mike noticed that he seemed to play better if he had a box of popcorn in his locker before a game. From then on, one of the Toronto trainer's jobs before a game was to get some popcorn into Palmateer's locker before he arrived. That wasn't the only superstition Mike held. After downing a box or two of popcorn, he sought out one of the assistant trainers to have his gloves slapped. Mike wouldn't go out onto the ice until this ritual was completed.

We usually think of superstitious people as being fearful or nervous, but Mike could hardly have been farther from that. The confident Palmateer would heckle opposing skaters during games, even as they were winding up to take a shot.

Palmateer can make the tough saves look easy and the easy ones look, well, unusual!

Just to keep things lively, he would pretend to be a radio announcer and give a play-by-play account of the action as it came toward him.

Naturally, much of this got on his opponents' nerves after a while, especially when Mike decided to entertain the crowd. Mike's showy style of play

44

caused people to accuse him of making the easy saves look difficult. Certainly there was no more acrobatic goalie in the NHL. Palmateer would spin, flop, dive, leap, slap at the puck, and even do the splits while stopping shots. Never one to stand still, he was constantly in and out of the net. Even during breaks in the action, he would take off his mask and skate around in circles.

Mike enjoyed the pressure of important games, but he could also be at his clowning best in the most ordinary practice. Whether he was punting pucks down the ice, batting them in the air with his stick, or throwing away his stick to guard the net with just his hands, Mike constantly kept things lively. Off the ice, he occasionally went out looking for some added danger to pack into his life. He scared himself silly swimming around in some shark-filled waters and nearly killed himself trying his luck at cliff diving.

Little Mike was a favorite with Toronto fans, but he had problems with the team's management. After being accused of faking an injury, Palmateer vowed to become a free agent and move on to another team at the end of the 1979-80 season. True to his word, he signed with the Washington Capitols. The Capitols had led an unlucky existence since being formed in 1974. Even with a play-off format that allowed 16 of the 21 teams to make the play-offs, the Capitols had never played in a post-season game. Palmateer couldn't change their luck; in fact, some of Washington's bad fortune rubbed off on him. Mike's goals-allowed average ballooned to 3.87 in 1980-81, and he sat out most of the next season with an injury.

The 1982-83 season found Mike traded back to his hometown Toronto Maple Leafs. Toronto's defense had fallen on hard times while Mike had been away. During the play-offs, his undermanned, injury-ridden team was outplayed by the heavily favored Minnesota North Stars. But Mike made sure the fans got their money's worth and showed he could still guard the goal as well as anyone in the game. Toronto won one game in the series, lost another by one goal, and forced the other two into overtime before losing. The North Stars, relieved to get out of Toronto with a win, claimed they had never seen a better job of goaltending. They were just another set of believers to add to Palmateer's growing list.

5
Mike
Liut

The St. Louis Blues discovered that in pro sports it is only a few short steps from the top of the heap to the bottom. St. Louis had been the most successful of the six expansion teams to enter the NHL in 1967. Seasoned with fine veterans, they had used a stubborn defense to gain the Stanley Cup finals in each of their first three years. The St. Louis players became popular, and sell-outs at Blues' games were common.

From then on, however, it was all downhill. During the 1970s, the Blues began to lose games more often, and they also lost fans and money. By 1976 the team had to cut way back on expenses to stay in business. Blues' players complained that management was so tight with money that they couldn't even get new sticks. During game

Liut flails at the puck in a last-ditch attempt to prevent a New York Ranger goal.

brawls, some St. Louis players would take advantage of the confusion to pick up sticks that their opponents had dropped on the ice!

That was the mess awaiting Mike Liut when he was asked to sign with the Blues in 1977. Mike was a 21-year-old goalie from Weston, Ontario. Like Esposito and Resch, he had left the Canadian junior leagues to attend college in the United States. While playing for Bowling Green University in Ohio, Mike first caught the eye of Emile Francis, the St. Louis general manager. Francis occasionally took time to watch the hockey games at St. Louis University and noticed the large Bowling Green goalie standing up to an endless volley of shots to keep his team in the game. Impressed, Francis made a note to keep track of Liut. After Mike was named player of the year in the Central Collegiate Hockey Association in 1976, Francis selected him in the fifth round of the draft.

Sadly for the Blues, though, they were determined to hold the line on spending in signing new players. Mike looked at their offer and the shaky state of the Blues' organization and turned them down. The Cincinnati Stingers of the World Hockey Association made him a better offer, and Mike suited up with them that year. The Stingers,

Mike Liut

however, proved to be no more stable than the Blues. Mike worked in the nets for two seasons with them without making much of an impression. When the WHA merged with the NHL in 1979, the Stingers quietly went out of business.

That left St. Louis with another chance to sign Mike, and this time they didn't let him escape. Emile Francis was so sure that Liut was the goalie he wanted that he dealt starting goaltender Phil Myre to Philadelphia before the 1979-80 season. That seemed like a risky move to the Blues' fans and players, most of whom had never heard of Liut. But they had to agree that, no matter who was in goal, the Blues could not get much worse than they already were. St. Louis had stumbled to a 20-47-13 mark in 1977-78 and then had dropped still farther to 18-50-12 the next year. Their once proud defense had vanished as they allowed a club record 348 goals in 1978-79, an average of almost 4½ per game.

Liut quickly won the starting job and set about mending the defense. Unusually large for a goalie, the 6-foot, 2-inch, 190-pound Liut reminded fans of another tall goalie, the great Ken Dryden. Mike used the same stand-up style as the ex-Montreal star. His long arms stabbed out to take away shots headed for the corners, and he was quick on his feet and used his legs well. Even off the ice, the intelligent, book-loving Liut seemed patterned after the law scholar Dryden.

Once St. Louis found what Mike could do in the net, they couldn't seem to resist playing him in nearly every game. In an age when almost all NHL teams alternated two goalies, Liut skated out to play game after game. Unlike St. Louis' ex-goalie Glenn Hall, who considered hockey to be 60 minutes of pure torture, Liut could hardly wait to go to work. He even ignored a common goalie tradition by going all out to stop shots in practice.

With their new goalie on the ice, the Blues looked like a different team. Mike cut more than a goal per game off the team average and allowed only 3.18 per contest. Appearing in 64 of the Blues' 80 games, he was on the ice for 32 wins and almost single-handedly pulled his team to a respectable 34-34-12 record in 1979-80.

But statistics told only part of the story. Liut had a knack for coming up with big saves when they were most needed. Francis claimed that no one could match his goalie in the last minutes of a closing game. Liut also inspired his teammates to play better. The Blues often started a game under heavy attack from their opponents. Liut would fend off the shots and suddenly come up with a spectacular save. That would spark both the Blues' players and fans to life. Confident that Mike could cover up for their mistakes, the players skated more aggressively and often turned the game around.

Also to Mike's advantage was the fact that he didn't fit the stereotype of the crazy goalie. Mike was an ordinary guy who worked at least as hard as everyone else. When he gave out advice and encouragement, people listened. His leadership helped the Blues in a game against the New York

The St. Louis Blues rally around their unmasked leader. Liut has been one of the few steady performers on a very unstable team.

Rangers in the 1980-81 season. After taking an early four-goal lead, the Blues started to take it easy. As the Blues relaxed, the Rangers buzzed around Liut and scored three uncontested goals. Liut stormed into the locker room at the end of the period and raged at his teammates. The Blues got the message. Playing a hard, close-checking game in the final period, they held off the Rangers for the win.

During 1981-82, Liut helped squeeze more wins out of the Blues' ordinary players than anyone thought possible. Only two years after they had lost 50 games in a season, St. Louis skated to a 45-18-17 mark, second only to the champion New York Islanders. Liut manned the nets for 61 of those games and recorded 33 wins. During the midseason All-Star game, Liut seemed to have clamped a lid on the goal. Playing half the game, he faced 25 shots from hockey's most skilled shooters and stopped all of them. There was no argument when he skated off with the game's Most Valuable Player Award. Liut came within one vote of winning the NHL's Hart Memorial Trophy as the league's Most Valuable Player for the season, but he lost out to Wayne Gretzky. It was the closest a goalie had come to winning the prize since 1962.

The Blues were unable to keep up their fine level of play for long, unfortunately. But even as the Blues fell back in the standings again, Liut proved his worth. During 1981-82, St. Louis finished 28-28-7 with Mike in goal. At the same time, they went through a streak of 21 straight games without a win when backup goalies took over. That proved, in bad times as well as good, the Blues' Iron Mike was their best hope to keep them in the game.

6
Andy
Moog

Andy Moog (pronounced Moag), who grew up in Penticton, British Columbia, knew what he was getting into when he chose to be a goalie. After all, his father had played the position well enough to help his amateur team, the Penticton Vees, to a championship in 1955. But nothing in his father's experience could possibly have prepared Andy for the dizzying ride up and down the ladder of fame that he rode in his first years in the NHL.

Moog's hockey career started peacefully enough when he was drafted by the Edmonton Oilers and sent to their farm team in 1980. There was nothing earthshaking about his performance at Wichita, Kansas. When he was called up to Edmonton near the end of the season, he saw action in only seven games and attracted little attention.

When it came to play-off time, Andy settled back to watch the Oilers' 10-year veteran goalie, Gary Edwards, battle the slick Montreal Canadiens. But a funny thing happened on the way to the Montreal Forum. Edmonton coach Glen Sather had been thinking about the grim situation that faced his club. Despite the presence of young superstar Wayne Gretzky, the Oilers had barely made the play-offs and finished 14th out of 21 teams in the NHL. Now they were up against hockey's most respected team, the Canadiens. Just two years ago, the Canadiens had swept to their fourth straight Stanley Cup title, and many of the stars of that team were still going strong. To make matters worse, the first two games of the best-of-five series had to be played in the Forum in front of the Canadiens' intimidating fans. What could Sather do to shake things up and even the odds? Incredibly, he looked over at his rookie goalie and asked if he wanted to play. When Moog saw that Sather was serious, he jumped at the chance.

That must have looked as if Edmonton was throwing in the towel before the series even started. The intense play-off pressure had wilted many fine goalies in the past; what would it do to a youngster who had been on the ice in only seven NHL games?

Andy skates behind his net to tee up the puck. By pulling the sliding puck away from the boards, Moog makes it easier for his teammates to break out of their own end.

Moog makes a kick save on a shot by the Philadelphia Flyers.

But with the help of Gretzky's puck-handling magic, Edmonton dominated play. Moog played a solid game in the nets, and the Oilers claimed a 6-3 win.

Embarrassed by their poor showing, a grim group of Canadiens stormed the Edmonton net at the start of the second game. Moog fought off the flurry of shots, but the Canadiens kept pressing. Finally, the puck bounced off a leg to a Canadien in front of the goal. With Moog caught guarding the other side of the net, the goal was wide open. The Montreal player shot the puck, and suddenly Moog flew across the net. His desperate lunge stopped the shot, leaving the Canadiens speechless as well as frustrated. Standing up to Montreal's furious attack, Moog helped his team to a 3-1 win. Edmonton then completed their upset with a 6-2 victory in Edmonton.

Moog went on to battle the tough New York Islanders and forced them to six games before finally bowing out. Along with Gretzky, the 5-foot, 9-inch goalie was the talk of the town. More than 50 stories about him came out in the Edmonton press in a single month. Because of his scrambling, stand-up, flop-down style of play, he was compared to Tony Esposito. Others said that his skill at controlling the puck reminded them of Ken Dryden.

Moog soaked up all the attention. As a result, he showed up at the Oilers' 1981 training camp with a big head and a bigger stomach. Out of shape and 20 pounds overweight, Moog impressed no one. The hero of a few months before found himself shipped back to Wichita. Moog's time in the minor leagues was made rougher by reports of a sensational new goalie on the team. Rookie Grant Fuhr had won over the Oiler fans as quickly as Moog had the year before. Minding the nets for 23 games without losing, Fuhr earned a spot on the second All-Star team.

The brash Oilers coasted to their divisional title in the NHL's new alignment. Brimming with confidence, they expected to wipe out the lowly Los Angeles Kings in the first round of the play-offs. But suddenly Edmonton's defense fell apart. They even blew a five-goal lead in one game, and the Kings knocked them out of the play-offs.

Moog returned to the Oilers in 1982, a better and wiser goaltender than when he had left. Although Edmonton's wide-open style of offensive hockey left them open to easy scores, their defense slowly improved as the season went on. The main reason was the play of Moog, who had beaten out Fuhr as the team's top goalie. The little guy's confidence won over his teammates, and they worked harder at keeping the opposition away from the nets.

On February 27, 1983, Andy gave Edmonton fans a rare treat. Stopping 25 shots, he shut out

Andy is a key figure in the Oilers' battle to unseat the Islanders (attacking above) as hockey's best team.

the Winnipeg Jets, 3-0. That was the Oilers' first shutout in their last 279 games! Moog finished the year with a 33-8-7 record to rank number two in wins and fifth in percent of shots blocked.

With more determination and better play in the nets from Moog, the Oilers crushed their opening foes in the 1983 play-offs. After a fine series against Winnipeg, Andy gave the Calgary Flames fits. The frustrated Flames were overwhelmed by Edmonton, and that left only Chicago blocking the Oilers' road

Moag played flawlessly in the 1983 semifinal against Chicago. Here he pokes the puck away from Black Hawk Tom Lysiak.

to the Stanley Cup finals. The Oilers embarrassed the highly rated Black Hawks with two easy wins in Edmonton. Heading into Chicago, they knew the Black Hawks would try to make up for their losses with a top effort. In game three, they gave it their best shot and sprayed the Edmonton goal with shots. Andy snuffed out all scoring chances for two periods and stopped 39 shots in Edmonton's 3-2 win.

Paced by Andy's 11-1 record and 2.77 goals-allowed average in the play-offs, Edmonton moved on to the finals. But they could not slow the New York Islanders' rush to a fourth straight title. Although Moog played well at times (letting in only one goal in the first game), New York's Billy Smith played far better. But at only 23 years of age, Andy Moog had already completed an impressive comeback. Both he and the Oilers hoped that his wild ride through the NHL had finally ended and that he could stay near the top for years to come.

Richard Brodeur shows how to protect the net during a face-off deep in his own end of the rink.

7
Richard Brodeur

Goaltending can be a frenzied job at the best of times. But when it comes to the Stanley Cup play-offs, the goalie is really on the spot. Some coaches claim that as much as 80 percent of a team's play-off success depends on the goalie. They note that even a team that totally controls the game can't win if they can't beat the last defender. That is one reason why the Stanley Cup games have had such a rich history of upsets. That one hot goalie can turn everything upside down.

There may be no goalie who has carried his team farther in the play-offs than Richard Brodeur. Although one of the smallest men in pro sports at 5 feet, 7 inches and 170 pounds, there is enough of him to shield a net, as the NHL discovered in 1982. That spring the Vancouver goalie played so brilliantly that he carried his mediocre club to the Stanley Cup finals. That incredible streak turned an almost unknown goalie into "King Richard."

Brodeur was born in Longueuil, Quebec, in 1952. Even as a young goalie, he had an unusually calm and easygoing manner. The only touchy thing about him was his reflexes, which kept him moving up the ranks of Canadian junior hockey. Richard joined the Cornwall Royals in the Quebec Junior Hockey League in 1970-71. Within a year, he had stopped enough shots to win an award as the league's best goalie.

It was a good time to make the jump into the pros with the new World Hockey Association bidding against the NHL for players. Although a seventh-round draft choice of the New York Islanders in 1972, Brodeur signed with Quebec of the WHA. There he gradually worked his way into the starting lineup and won a regular job in 1974-75. His 69 starts that season made him one of the busiest goalies in the game. With their wide-open style of play, the offensive-minded Nordiques left Richard to handle many tough shots.

Brodeur played seven years in the WHA until it finally disbanded in 1979. That year he was reclaimed by the Islanders. But it was soon obvious

Richard Brodeur

that the Islanders had no use for him. With Billy Smith and Chico Resch already battling for playing time and promising youngster Roland Melanson waiting for a chance, Richard spent his time on the sidelines. The fourth-string goalie got into only two games in 1979-80. As the next season approached, Richard sensed that the Islanders would send him to the minors, and he was prepared to retire rather than accept that fate.

But on October 6, 1980, two days before the opening game, New York practically gave Richard away to the Vancouver Canucks. All they asked in return was an exchange of fifth-round draft picks. Brodeur didn't expect to see much action in

A good goalie must not only stop the first shot; he must also see that his opponents do not get a rebound chance. Here Brodeur faces that challenge against the Winnipeg Jets.

Vancouver, either, when Glen Hanlon was known as one of the NHL's best young goalies. But Hanlon suffered an injury that year, and that forced the Canucks to turn to Brodeur. Surprisingly, Richard played well enough for Vancouver to trade Hanlon to St. Louis.

Tucked away in the northwest corner of the continent, Vancouver had been fighting for years to gain recognition in the league. But the Canucks had a very ordinary team with no stars. Even their strange uniforms with bright yellow, orange, and black vees brought only snickers. In 1981-82 they had muddled to a typical 30-33-17 record to finish 11th among the 21 NHL teams.

In the first round of the 1982 play-offs, the Calgary Flames outskated the Canucks throughout most of the series. But Brodeur made such lightning stops it almost looked as though he were playing at a different speed than all the other players. The baffled Flames went down to defeat in three straight games.

Next came the Los Angeles Kings, fresh from a high-scoring shootout with the Edmonton Oilers. Again, Brodeur was nearly perfect as the Canucks stopped the Kings, four games to one. Then in the semifinals against the Chicago Black Hawks, Brodeur seemed to have set up a magnetic force field in front of the net. He began the series by blocking 46 Black Hawk shots, holding Chicago to one goal, and forcing the game into overtime. With "King Richard," as the press had begun to call him, keeping Chicago at bay, Vancouver finally pulled out a 2-1 win in two overtimes. After moving ahead three games to one, Vancouver let Richard finish off the series with a flourish. He stopped all but two of the 38 Black Hawk shots in posting a 6-2 win.

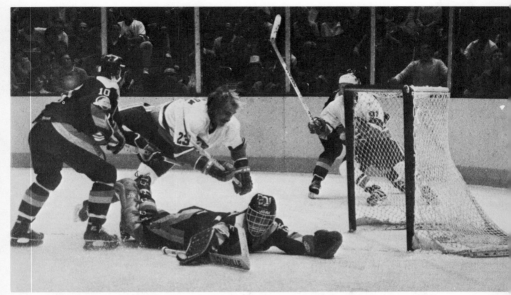

In the 1982 Stanley Cup finals, Brodeur made Islanders like Bob Nystrom (23) work hard for their goals.

Vancouver's opponent in the finals, the New York Islanders, was so superior a team that the series should have been a joke. The only thing that made it interesting was the fact that Brodeur was doing a superhuman job. In the first three rounds of play-off action, he helped his team to an 11-2 mark, despite the fact the Canucks were outshot in eight of those games. Brodeur continued to amaze fans with his play against New York, but the Islanders had too much firepower. In the first game, Brodeur and his teammates sent the game into overtime,

but they finally lost on a foolish play by a defenseman that allowed New York to score with two
seconds left in the period.

That one goal seemed to spoil the Brodeur magic,
and the Canucks went down to defeat in three
straight games. But his long play-off streak had
turned Brodeur into a star. Suddenly he commanded
a top salary and was considered one of the top
goalies in the game. Now the Canucks wouldn't
think of letting him go. With a goalie like Brodeur,
you never know when your team might strike it rich.

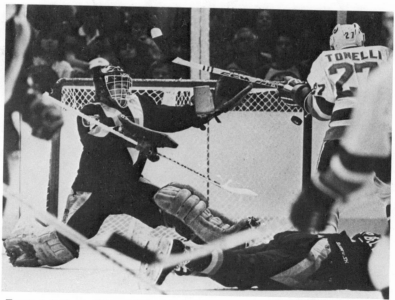

Even a hot goalie can't hold out forever. Steady pressure by the
Islanders has led to a goal in the upper right-hand corner of the net.

From November 13, 1982, to February 13, 1983, Peeters did not lose a game. His record during that stretch was 26 wins, 0 losses, and 5 ties.

8
Pete
Peeters

The Boston Bruins' goalie decided that the tradition had gone on long enough. There had been a Peter Peeters in the family since long before he was born, with his father, grandfather, and great-grandfather going by that unusual name. But goalie Peeters, the youngest of the line, had gotten tired of it and has vowed not to pass the name along to his sons. And when Pete decides to put a stop to something, the issue is closed. Just ask any number of pro hockey's top scorers who have tried to slip a puck past his pads.

Pete was born in Edmonton, Alberta, in 1957. Like many pro goalies, he did not win rave reviews for his play as a youngster. In fact, Peeters was far more interested in a swimming career and did not play junior hockey until he was 18. He allowed

Pete Peeters

more than four goals per game while playing for the Medicine Hat (Alberta) Tigers and lasted until the eighth round of the 1977 draft before he was claimed by the Philadelphia Flyers. From there Pete took the low road to fame, spending two years with minor league teams in Milwaukee and Maine before gaining a brief trial with the Flyers in 1978-79. The Flyers liked what they saw and promoted him to the big leagues.

As soon as Pete took over the nets in 1979-80, Philadelphia must have wondered why they hadn't called on him earlier. Pete was like a four-leaf clover to the team and brought them an incredible streak of luck. For week after week, the Flyers could not lose as long as the rookie was playing. Peeters kept his unbeaten string going for 27 games, only 5 short of the all-time record of 32 held by Boston's Gary Cheevers.

With a fine 2.73 goals-against average, Peeters took over much of the play-off load from veteran

There is no tougher test for a goalie than facing a superstar roaring in alone on a breakaway. Here Peeters stopped New York's Bryan Trottier in the finals of the 1980 Stanley Cup play-offs.

75

goalie Phil Myre. He held up well against the Stanley Cup pressure and allowed only 2.78 goals per game. Philadelphia moved into the finals against the New York Islanders but came up just short. Pete, who was in the Flyer net for the final loss in the hard-fought, six-game series, took the defeats hard. After the game, he hauled a chair into the shower and sat there silently brooding over the lost championship.

Brooding was just one of Peeters' many moods. He has been ejected for yelling at officials and has gotten into his share of scrapes with opponents in front of the net. But even though he was tagged with the nickname "Grumpy" from the press, Peeters got along well with the skaters. He helped the team to take pride in good defensive work and made sure to congratulate all of his teammates when he recorded a shutout.

At 6 feet and 170 pounds, Peeters was taller and leaner than the average netminder. In 1980-81 he showed that he was also quite a bit better than average. The second-year man again helped the Flyers stay near the top by allowing fewer than three goals per game.

The Flyer goalie seemed to develop a leak in 1981-82, however. His average soared to 3.71 goals per game, and the Flyers were quick to give up on him. They tried to trade him away, but for a long time it seemed that no one else was interested in him. Finally, the Boston Bruins offered defenseman Brad McCrimmon in exchange, and the Flyers accepted. Pete had always been especially tough against the Bruins, and they hoped that he could bounce back.

Peeters did more than bounce back in 1982-83; he skyrocketed into fame. Boston's tight forechecking limited opponents to about 25 shots per game, and

As Pete shows against the New England Whalers, a goalie on a winning streak can seem to change directions in midair.

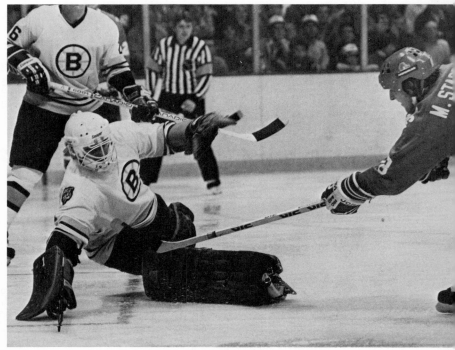

Pete lunges after a shot by Quebec's Marian Stastny.

Pete had little trouble stopping those. During one winter stretch, Peeters seemed to have declared the goal off limits to everyone. Three of the four teams he faced during that time—Buffalo, Quebec, and the New York Rangers—all came up empty on the scoreboard. That matched Pete's shutout total in his first three years combined!

Not even the dreaded Islanders could beat Peeters in the regular season. The three-time defending

Stanley Cup champs scored only three goals in three games against him as they lost two of the games and tied one.

Pete's goals-against average of 2.36 was far below the rest of the league, and he easily led the NHL in wins with a 40-11-9 mark. Then Pete took off on another lucky streak and came within 1 game of Gary Cheever's 32-game unbeaten streak. Those totals, along with his league-leading eight shutouts, helped earn his third All-Star honor in four years and turned the Flyers' orange team colors red with embarrassment.

Best of all for the Bruins was the way Peeters could keep his team in almost every game. Often a team that gets a quick goal can pull away from an NHL opponent. Pete saw that few teams got the jump on Boston as he posted an incredible 30 first-period shutouts. With such solid backing from their goalie, the Bruins cruised to a 50-20-10 record, the best in the league.

Unfortunately, Pete could not come close to matching his regular season form in the play-offs. Still, there were a few bright moments, such as his shutout over Buffalo in the quarterfinals. But far more glaring were the three goals he allowed in one period to Quebec's Peter Stastny and the pounding he took from the Islanders in the semifinals. The New York team that Pete had handcuffed all year broke loose for a flood of goals to put the Bruins out of the play-offs in six games.

In the future, Peeters will get other chances to prove that he can handle the pressure of play-off goaltending. But it may be a long time before any goalie can match the regular-season job he did in 1982-83. In finishing second to Wayne Gretzky in the voting for the NHL's Most Valuable Player Award, Pete Peeters showed that he ranked with the best in the game.